AF256834

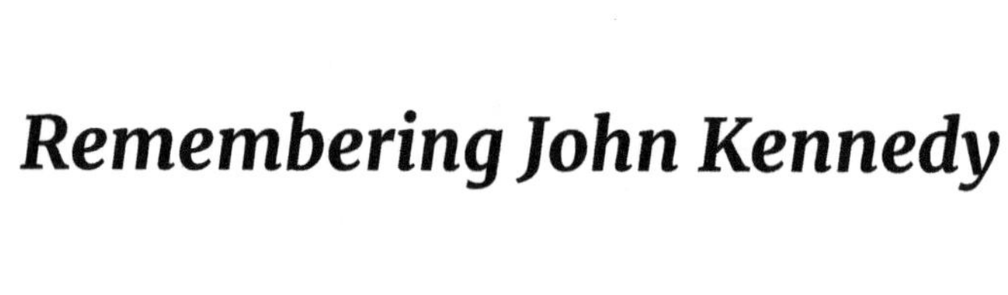
Remembering John Kennedy

To order additional copies of this book, contact:

Maple Leaf Publishing Inc.
3rd Floor 4915 54 Street Red Deer, Alberta T4N 2G7, Canada
1-(403)-356-0255

Cover creation : Frédéric Bar

Layout : Frédéric Bar

Table des matières

Introduction :

In memory of John Kennedy

My first memory is of then Senator John Fitzgerald Kennedy at the Democratic Convention in July 1956. After the convention, political apathy for me set in again.

My next memory is of him as a candidate for the Democrat nomination for presidency. H seemed like a breath of fresh air compared to the national figures I had seen on television and read about in newspapers.

I was enthused and proud of my party and inspired by this man I believed would be the next president and my new commander-in-chief.

His death was truly one of the seminal moments in my life, but his inspiration still lives in me.

Chapter 1 – Democratic Convention 1956

In July 1956, I watched the Democratic Convention. I was not a political nerd, but I was intrigued by the speeches and events that was the nomination process. There, I first saw Senator John Fitzgerald Kennedy when he placed Governor Stevenson's name in nomination as the Democrat candidate of the Democrat party.

''The time is ripe. The hour has struck. The man is here; and he is ready. Let the word go forth that we have fulfilled our responsibility to the nation. Ladies and gentlemen of the convention: it is now my privilege to present to this convention, as candidate for President of the United States, the name of the man uniquely qualified – by virtue of his compassion, his conscience, and his courage – to follow in the great traditions of Jefferson, Jackson, Wilson, Roosevelt, and the man from Independence. Fellow Delegates, I give you the man from Libertyville – the next Democratic nominee and the next President of the United States – Adlai E. Stevenson.''

This was the convention where the presidential candidate, Governor Adlai Stevenson did not select his vice-president but turned to the convention to choose between the top two choices, Senators John Kennedy and Estes Kefauver.

Senator Kennedy actively sought the VP post, certainly without the enthusiastic support of his family, and apparently in the belief that President Eisenhower might not run for re-election because of health issues. His intentions were two terms as a loyal vice-president and then his own terms as president. The general election in 1956 certainly would have been different without President Eisenhower on the ticket.

Throwing the convention open to select the VP created chaos and generated a miniature campaign season that would last hours with smoked filled rooms taking place on the convention floor. Both candidates had supporters and detractors and while Stevenson had a preference, apparently for Senator Kennedy, he did not make his views known. The decision was not made until after the second roll call vote with Kefauver leading the first role call and Kennedy the second roll call. In the background votes were changing and Senator Kennedy asked to address the convention. Speaker Rayburn let him speak and he withdrew his name from consideration and asked that Senator Kefauver be unanimously selected as the vice-presidential candidate. It was a short speech, just a few words that I don't remember but words that had a magnetic effect on me and I was an instant convert to a John F. Kennedy fan. The power of that speech and the nominating speech was not the words, but the inspiration of John F. Kennedy. He thanked the convention for its generosity and kindness.

He added that the day's action had demon-strated the party's strength and unity and the "good judgment" of Mr. Stevenson in bringing the Vice-Presidential issue to the floor instead of hand-picking his successor, as has been the custom. He spoke of Senator Kefauver as a tireless cam-paigner that would make an admirable running mate for Mr. Stevenson. "I move we suspend the rules and make this nomination by acclamation," said Senator Kennedy. Speaker Rayburn called for the "ayes" and the crowd roared its approval.

That was the smart thing for Senator Kennedy to do for his political future. Senator John F. Kennedy's popularity with the public was well deserved and earned. When he set out across the country to cam-paign for Adlai Stevenson that summer, his charm, wit, and humor left audiences clamoring for more. Eisenhower did run for reelection and had a com-manding lead in the polls with Stevenson likely to lose the election by a landslide. Senator Kennedy realized that campaigning for Stevenson was an effective way to boost his own recognition across the country for any future campaign. Kennedy traveled to twenty-four states and gave about 150 speech-es before the November election, which went, as expected, to Eisenhower. For Kennedy, the intensity of campaigning for Stevenson was a learning ex-perience that gave him a glimpse of what his own future campaign would entail. A perhaps bigger advantage was that he was not part of a "second defeat" by Eisenhower-Nixon. After the Democrat Convention and election were over, I went back to my political indifference for the next four years.

I may have been indifferent, but Senator John Kennedy was anything but indifferent. He actively campaigned for the Stevenson-Kefauver ticket around the United States. He established his credibility that would serve him well four years later.

Chapter 2 - JFK Announces Candidacy for President

On January 2, 1960 Senator John F. Kennedy announced his candidacy for president of the United States. He stated his view of the office, "the most powerful office in the Free World" the power of the office, "the most important decision facing the world must be made here," and the issues he considered most important: "the arms race with the Soviet Union, freedom and order in newly emerging nations, science and education in the United States an economic growth to benefit all Americans.

He stated his intentions to run on the issues he listed and his belief that Americans needed to make their choice on the issues and that he would present his positions on the issues to Americans in primary contests.He viewed the 1960 election for presidency as significant for the United States as the election of 1932 and the importance of electing a Democrat as president in both. He also stated his qualifications to be the next president.

"For 18 years, I have been in the service of the United States, first as a naval officer in the Pacific during World War II and for the past 14 years as a member of the Congress. In the last 20 years, I have traveled in nearly every continent and country -- from Leningrad to Saigon, from Bucharest to Lima.

From all of this, I have developed an image of America as fulfilling a noble and historic role as the defender of freedom in a time of maximum peril -- and of the American people as confident, courageous and persevering. It is with this image that I begin this campaign."

To me the choice was obvious – how can you not pick this young energetic and charismatic future leader? But the choice was not up to me, I wasn't even old enough to vote either to choose the Democrat candidate, John Kennedy, or anoint him as president.

My totally irrelevant choice was made; however, the Democrat party choice was still up in the air with seven major candidates, four actively campaigning plus favorite sons with three of the major candidates essentially hoping for a contested convention. Senator Kennedy, my leader of the future, was seen by many Democratic Party elders as "too youthful and inexperienced" to be president and perhaps he should be the vice-presidential candidate. Senator Kennedy recognized this as an effort to deny him status as a major candidate and flatly stated, "I am not running for vice-president, I am running for president."

Chapter 3 - Democratic Campaign

Let the campaign began! An early step was Senator Kennedy challenging and defeating Senator Humphrey in the Wisconsin primary. A win with an asterisk. His margin of victory came from Catholic areas plus the entire Kennedy clan invading Wisconsin and searching for votes. This gave a slimmer of hope to Senator Humphrey and he continued to West Virginia, a more favorable state to him as a majority Protestant state. A televised debate was held in West Virginia between Senators Humphrey and Kennedy with Kennedy winning the debate. Senator Humphrey's campaign was swamped by the well-funded and organized Kennedy campaign. In the primary, Kennedy won with over 60% of the vote. This was double victory, he won the vote and demonstrated that he, as a Catholic, could win Protestant votes. 56 years later, 2016, every state has a process to cast votes for a candidate, either a primary or caucus. In 1960 Senator Kennedy only competed in nine primaries, nine more than his rivals. Following the primaries, Kennedy traveled around the nation speaking to state delegations and their leaders. As the Democratic Convention opened, Kennedy was far in the lead, but was still short of the delegate total needed to win the nomination. Days before the convention opened, Senator Lyndon Johnson and Governor Adlai Stevenson announced their candidacy for president.

Senator Johnson challenged Senator Kennedy to a televised debate in front of a joint meeting of the Texas and Massachusetts delegations. Kennedy accepted and the general view was that he won the debate. Johnson generated little support outside of the South. Stevenson had significant support from liberal delegates, but two landslide defeats meant there was a desire for a new face with a better chance of victory.

Senator Kennedy's health was questioned by supporters of Senator Johnson, but that was essentially denied and went nowhere. In reality he did have numerous and serious health issues that were covered up thoroughly. Consequently, the voters had no idea of John Kennedy's health and how that might affect his ability to perform as president. Certainly it was not an issue in 1960 and John Fitzgerald Kennedy became the Democratic candidate for president of the United States.

Chapter 4 - Accepting the Nomination

On July 15, 1960 Senator John F. Kennedy accepted the Democratic Nomination for the Presidency of the United States. To fully appreciate the inspiration of John Kennedy to me as he presented his views, I have included the points that did and still stand out in my mind.

With a deep sense of duty and high resolve, I accept your nomination.
I accept it with a full and grateful heart--without reservation-- and with only one obligation--the obligation to devote every effort of body, mind and spirit to lead our Party back to victory and our Nation back to greatness.
For I stand tonight facing west on what was once the last frontier. From the lands that stretch three thousand miles behind me, the pioneers of old gave up their safety, their comfort and sometimes their lives to build a new world here in the West. They were not the captives of their own doubts, the prisoners of their own price tags. Their motto was not "every man for himself"--but "all for the common cause." They were determined to make that new world strong and free, to overcome its hazards and its hardships, to conquer the enemies that threatened from without and within.

Today some would say that those struggles are all over--that all the horizons have been explored-- that all the battles have been won-- that there is no longer an American frontier.

But I trust that no one in this vast assemblage will agree with those sentiments. For the problems are not all solved, and the battles are not all won--and we stand today on the edge of a New Frontier-- the frontier of the 1960's--a frontier of unknown opportunities and perils-- a frontier of unfulfilled hopes and threats.

But the New Frontier of which I speak is not a set of promises--it is a set of challenges. It sums up not what I intend to offer the American people, but what I intend to ask of them. It appeals to their pride, not to their pocketbook--it holds out the promise of more sacrifice instead of more security.

But I tell you the New Frontier is here, whether we seek it or not. Beyond that frontier are the uncharted areas of science and space, unsolved problems of peace and war, unconquered pockets of ignorance and prejudice, unanswered questions of poverty and surplus. It would be easier to shrink back from that frontier, to look to the safe mediocrity of the past, to be lulled by good intentions and high rhetoric--and those who prefer that course should not cast their votes for me, regardless of party – to me absolutely no complacency.

But I believe the times demand new invention, innovation, imagination, decision. I am asking each of you to be pioneers on that New Frontier. My call is to the young in heart, regardless of age--to all who respond to the Scriptural call: "Be strong and of a good courage; be not afraid, neither be thou dismayed."

For courage--not complacency--is our need to-day--leadership--not salesmanship. And the only valid test of leadership is the ability to lead and lead vigorously. A tired nation, said David Lloyd George, is a Tory nation--and the United States today cannot afford to be either tired or Tory. There may be those who wish to hear more--more promises to this group or that--more harsh rhetoric about the men in the Kremlin--more assurances of a golden future, where taxes are always low and subsidies ever high. But my promises are in the platform you have adopted--our ends will not be won by rhetoric and we can have faith in the future only if we have faith in ourselves. For the harsh facts of the matter are that we stand on this frontier at a turning-point in history. We must prove all over again whether this nation--or any nation so conceived--can long endure--whether our society--with its freedom of choice, its breadth of opportunity, its range of alternatives--can compete with the single-minded advance of the Communist system. Can a nation organized and governed such as ours endure? That is the real question. Have we the nerve and the will? Can we carry through in an age where we will witness not only new breakthroughs in weapons of destruction--but also a race for mastery of the sky and the rain, the ocean and the tides, the far side of space and the inside of men's minds? Are we up to the task--are we equal to the challenge? Are we willing to match the Russian sacrifice of the present for the future--or must we sacrifice our future in order to enjoy the present?

That is the question of the New Frontier. That is the choice our nation must make--a choice that lies not merely between two men or two parties, but between the public interest and private comfort--between national greatness and national decline--between the fresh air of progress and the stale, dank atmosphere of "normalcy"--between determined dedication and creeping mediocrity. All mankind waits upon our decision. A whole world looks to see what we will do. We cannot fail their trust; we cannot fail to try - to me doing nothing was losing.

It has been a long road from that first snowy day in New Hampshire to this crowded convention city. Now begins another long journey, taking me into your cities and homes all over America. Give me your help, your hand, your voice, your vote. Recall with me the words of Isaiah: "They that wait upon the Lord shall renew their strength; they shall mount up with wings as eagles; they shall run and not be weary."

As we face the coming challenge, we too, shall wait upon the Lord, and ask that he renew our strength. Then shall we be equal to the test. Then we shall not be weary. And then we shall prevail.

Chapter 5 – Presidential Campaign

One issue remained that could destroy his dream – the religious issue. On September 12, 1960 Senator addressed the issue directly in a speech to the Greater Houston Ministerial Association. He acknowledged the importance of the religious issue and also pointed out there were far more pressing issues facing the United States, the spread of Communism 90 miles off the coast of Florida, poverty, people unable to pay medical bills, families losing their farms, too many slums, too few schools and too late to the moon and outer space – war hunger and despair know no religious barriers.

He stressed the point that he was an American first and as a military member, Representative and Senator had taken and followed an oath to support and defend the constitution, that as president his first priority was to the Constitution of the United States, not Papal decree. He pointed out that he served his country in war and his brother died in war as Americans. He challenged America to end religious intolerance. He challenged Americans to judge him based on his record of service, military and congress and that he was the "Democratic" candidate for president, not the Catholic candidate. Kennedy emphasized that in the most remote possibility that he had to choose between violating his conscience or the national interest that he would resign and not do anything to jeopardize the national interest.

Kennedy also offered no apology for his views and that he had no intention of disavowing either his religion or church to win the election. He essentially said, this is who I am, this is who I will be, a loyal American that served his country in war and peace, that I will faithfully and fully honor my oath of office. Ultimately it is hard to judge how much, if any, his religion affected the election, but he addressed it directly and there was little else he could do.

Senator Kennedy campaigned enthusiastically on the issues he felt important – basically America No 1 in space, in defense, education, science, economics and defending freedom around the world from Communism. He refused to accept there were no new frontiers to explore and challenged Americans with a New Frontier – a mystical future of unknown achievement – a Valhalla of human potential.
He laid out clear choices between himself and Vice-president Nixon with Nixon saying America had never had it so good and Senator Kennedy challenging America to do better. Senator Kennedy emphasized many times the importance of the decisions Americans would be making in 1960 – either continue the status quo or go forward into that New Frontier of new challenges not promises.

The 1960 presidential election was the closest election since 1916 in the popular vote but not the electoral college, which can be explained by a number of factors.

Kennedy benefitted from the economic recession of 1957–58, which hurt the standing of the incumbent Republican Party, and he had the advantage of 17 million more registered Democrats than Republicans. Furthermore, the new votes that Kennedy gained among Catholics almost neutralized the new votes Nixon gained among Protestants which indicated that the ghost of Catholicism was not dead. Kennedy's campaigning skills decisively outmatched Nixon's. In the debates Kennedy just looked better, more confident, more like a leader. In the end, Nixon's emphasis on his experience carried little weight, and he wasted energy by campaigning in all 50 states instead of concentrating on the swing states. Kennedy used his large, well-funded campaign organization to win the nomination, secure endorsements, and, with the aid of the last of the big-city bosses, get out the vote in the big cities. He relied on running mate Lyndon B. Johnson to hold the South, and used television effectively.

Chapter 6 – Elected President

President Kennedy assumed office facing threats and problems around the world, both close to home and on the opposite side of the world.

The Bay of Pigs fiasco was enough of a problem in its own right, but it also put President Kennedy in the position of confronting a "bullying" Khrushchev from a position of weakness. Khrushchev implied a threat of a unilateral solution to Berlin. To his credit President Kennedy did not back down from this threat but there was an escalation of threats with potential for serious consequences – and late that year construction of the "Berlin Wall" began. Southeast Asia was a potential hotspot since the end of WWII. The colonial powers wanted an immediate return of their colonies while these nations wanted independence. President Roosevelt preferred free nations, even if that meant opposing an ally during the war, France.   His death, combined with the reality that the situation in Europe in confronting an actively expanding USSR seemed far more serious then situation in Cambodia, Laos and Vietnam.

Paranoia about communism was also a factor, especially Communism USSR – style, which was a legitimate concern and required legitimate action, but political rhetoric led to statements and decisions that in the long run were counter-productive.

A proposal was made, allegedly by Russia, that BOTH North and South Vietnam be admitted to the United Nations. This certainly would have changed to picture in Southeast Asia but that would require the United States to recognize a new communist nation – something that John Foster Dulles was incapable of doing.

In the 1960 election, Vietnam, Laos and Cambodia were issues that were relegated to "almost there" by the threat of Communism, United States pride as number one strategically, economically and in space.

President Kennedy essentially continued the policies of President's Truman and Eisenhower in containing communism in Southeast Asia with military advisors with perhaps questionable limits on the actual duties. Did they engage in or lead ARVN forces in combat?

The crisis in Southeast Asia did increase but I do not remember it as ever a serious issue for President Kennedy. As the situation deteriorated, Vietnam became known as "McNamara's War." It was obvious covert operations were taking place, but whatever was carried out was kept well hidden from the American public and certainly not a serious issue during President Kennedy's term.

In 1961 weather forecasters began receiving orders to Vietnam. The orders were to Headquarters First Weather Wing at Yokota AB, pending further assignment – which meant the orders were physically to South Vietnam.

A key mission of weather forecaster is supporting air and artillery operations which leads question, why were they there and supporting ARVN or U.S. air and artillery operations? There were also military personnel from all parts of Japan that performed temporary duty in South Vietnam.

In 1962, the economy was threatened by a steel strike and president Kennedy did not want to see a rerun of the 1959 steel strike. A point made by President Kennedy was that pay increases should be based on productivity. A labor contract was going nowhere, and the administration intervened. An agreement was mediated that called for an increase in fringe benefits with no wage hikes that year and an unstated principle that there would be no price increases. Roger Blough, U.S. Steel CEO met with President Kennedy and said that US Steel was raising its price and other companies would follow this lead.
President Kennedy was incensed by this and said bad things about Roger Blough – including questioning the legitimacy of his parentage. President Kennedy rightly saw this as a double cross and used every bit of U.S. government influence including switching DOD contracts to steel companies not raising prices. The price increase was rolled back, and President Kennedy used the influence of the presidency to achieve results benefiting the economy. By 1963 the situation in South Vietnam needed to be resolved with a regime change in South Vietnam virtually required.

An active plan by President Kennedy, his administration and ARVN generals called for a coup to remove Ngo Din Diem from power and send him into exile. Ngo Dinh Diem and his brother Ngo Diem Nhu were assassinated with the approval of the ARVN generals. I do not believe it is accurate to say the US government approved the deaths, but certainly the coup was supported at the highest US government level. Regardless of reality, there was a strong implication the deaths were approved by the United States.

The civil rights campaign was certainly an issue during President Kennedy's tenure and his record can be seen as checkered. It was an issue during the 1960 election and Senator Kennedy campaigned on a strong civils rights program. Once elected President Kennedy seemed to have changed his priorities, however that ignores the reality that advancements were subject to the politics of the time. It is certain that President Kennedy was a legitimate and strong believer in civil rights, but even the belief of a youthful leader could not completely overpower the political reality of the times. In 1962, President Kennedy sent US Marshalls to enforce a court order admitting James Meredith to the University of Mississippi. In February 1962, President Kennedy submitted a civil rights bill to congress that he did little to support and it floundered in congress.

In May 1963, President Kennedy proposed a broad new civil rights bill described as the most sweeping civil rights legislation since Reconstruction with the potential to be a critical political mistake.

On June 11, 1963 while Governor Wallace stood in the school house door, President Kennedy made a powerful speech in support of his legislation and calling for all American's to support this legislation. To America he said, "We are confronted primarily with a moral issue. It is as old as the scriptures and is as clear as the American Constitution. The heart of the question is whether all Americans are to be afforded equal rights and equal opportunities." This makes civil rights an issue where the paths of President Kennedy's intentions are clear with his record of accomplishments muddy and his last and greatest effort put into effect by his successor.

It has to be admitted that the Cuban Missile Crisis fed the Bay of Pigs and subsequent events, such as the confrontation with Khrushchev where the president was alternatively lectured and threatened. Khrushchev did follow through on his threat to solve the Belin situation unilaterally by beginning construction of the Berlin Wall. He then started moving offensive bombers and tactical nuclear missiles into Cuba. Russia obviously denied accusations that they were moving nuclear weapons into Cuba. The United States had reconnaissance information proving there were missiles in Cuba. In the United Nations there was the picture of the United States Ambassador to the united Nations, Adlai Stephenson, challenging the Russian Ambassador and said, "He was prepared for hell to freeze over for an answer." For JFK, the embarrassment of the Bay of Pigs was in part caused by his indecisive leadership, but here he did make clear decisions.

Two options presented by his advisors were air strikes or an invasion. President Kennedy overruled both and chose an embargo to prevent further delivery of missiles while they bought time to negotiate and the missiles eventually were removed. There was some secret negotiations and secret deals made that achieved success in removing a nuclear threat less than one hundred miles from the United States. Was this the only way that threat could have been resolved? Was it a confrontation provoked by the publicity from the United States. The missile crisis was an achievement for JFK but was it a public confrontation caused in part by verbosity of the JFK Administration? How much were the words and action of each side influenced by the words and threats after the Bay of Pigs and the confrontation between a less confident President Kennedy and a confident and intimidating Premier Khrushchev.

I was stationed at Misawa AB on northern Honshu and all we knew was what was broadcast on AFRTS and that information was far from complete and very much the same each day. I do not remember very much hope for a peaceful solution, listening to Armed Forces Radio and Television broadcast of the situation as it unfolded in the Caribbean. I have no idea of what was live when I heard it, but I was also influenced by comment of Air Forces officers at the Supervisor of Flying position when they made comments based on their positions and experience. During the Cuban Missile crisis, it was as close as I have ever felt that a total war was possible, even probable with a sense that could include death.

The Russian ships carrying the nuclear weapons were headed for Cuba and the U.S. Navy forming a blockade in international water to prevent that delivery. The thought in my mind was what would happen, how would the world survive, how would I survive. Then there was such a sense of relief when the information was broadcast that the Russian ships were returning to Russian waters.

The question for me, now and then is, how close to Armageddon were we?

Chapter 7 – Assassination

After the missile crisis was over, life on Japan at least pretty much went back to normal. American advisors were still advising/training/leading ARVN forces? Buddhist monks continued to protest the policies of Diem and monks continued to die by immolation. I was aware that was happening but for whatever reason this issue was covered much more in the United States than Japan. These events certainly were factors that caused President Kennedy to drop his support of Ngo Dinh Diem.

My Detachment had an early Christmas party on Nov 22, 1963 starting at 7 PM Japan time, or 4 AM in Dallas. Our function ended at about 10 PM Japan time or 7 AM Dallas time. Presidential party activities, breakfast and a speech would soon start and for us in Japan our day was ending. Whether in Japan, waiting for a new day or anticipating the new day in the United States, shock, grief, or both would end the day for virtually everyone in the world. After the breakfast and a speech, the president and party flew to Love Field, greeted their fans and rode the motorcade on its route through down-town Dallas and Lee Harvey Oswald went to work in the Texas School Book Depository.

By approximately 12:30 the limousine had turned on Elm street and the target was in sight, the shooter in place. One basic fact is that three shots were fired from the sixth floor of the Texas School Book Depository.

The sound of three gunshots, the sound of the bolt operating three times and the sound of three spent rifle cartridges hit the floor above two employees on the fifth floor watching the parade. Another basic fact: Lee Harvey Oswald took a rifle to work disguised as he said curtain rods. Critics claim he carried nothing to work with him, but a fact is that his rifle was the one found on the sixth floor and had been fired. There was no last-minute route change. To get to the Stemmons Freeway there was a physical blockade between Main St and the entrance to the Stemmons. Because of that the limousine had to get onto Elm street to enter the Stemmons Freeway.

Whatever happened in Dealy Plaza, it happened one way and one way only, either one of the conspiracies or the official version of events. I accept the official version, but I do not argue in favor of that version and I do question many of the conspiracy theories. What I do believe happened is that of the three shots fired from the vicinity of the sixth floor of the Texas School Book Depository, one shot missed, one shot hit both President Kennedy and Gov. Connolly and one shot hit President Kennedy only.

Physical evidence demonstrates clearly that one bullet hit both men. First, the entrance wound on Gov. Connolly is blocked by President Kennedy's body. Second, the entrance wound on Gov. Connolly is a keyhole − the bullet is tumbling when it hits him and means the bullet went through something before it hit Connolly, President Kennedy's body.

The physical evidence indicates a small hole in the upper rear of President Kennedy's head and a big hole in the right front portion of his head. I saw a copy of the Zapruder film on a VCR tape and that copy indicated a vapor trail from above and the rear that hit Kennedy's head before it exploded.
Forensic experts have demonstrated that the type of weapon used by Oswald would give the results that happened to Kennedy's and Connolly's bodies.
An 85-year-old man demonstrated that the type of weapon Oswald used could be fired fast enough to make the shots fired by Oswald.

Concerning the conspiracies, where is the evidence that someone besides Oswald fired any weapon in Dealy Plaza on No 22, 1963? Who would hire some-one like Lee Harvey Oswald to shoot the president? One theory claims the throat wound was an en-trance wound. If so, where did that bullet come from without hitting Gov. Connolly's head? Another the-ory claims that the head shot came from the grassy knoll, in part because of the perceived movement of President Kennedy's head. However, a direct shot from the grassy knoll would have exited out the left side of Kennedy's head. That did not happen.

Regardless of how it happened, either one of the conspiracies or the official version of events, the consequences were and are the same. President Kennedy was dead, the future for his ardent fans shattered and Camelot came to life. In death he became this mythical figure at the insistence of Jacqueline Kennedy and the real John Kennedy is virtually shrouded from reality.

Chapter 8 Inspiration

It is easy to find vast amounts of information that describes the life and career of this man born John Fitzgerald Kennedy but what does that say about the man living in that body? What can anyone say about him to describe him? What can I say about him? I never met him, I never talked to him to understand his feelings and unguarded thoughts about issues? To quote Will Rogers, all I know is what I read in the papers and saw on television and all I have is my memories of the man that lived in the public eye.

I see parallels between the public service of John Kennedy and Pilgrims Progress, not an exact comparison but in general terms in the path followed – the straight and narrow for Pilgrim's Progress and accepting the challenges faced in life and the nation for John Kennedy. John Kennedy tended to see things as either, or, such as a free world or dominated by tyrants.

John Kennedy promised a future he defined as a New Frontier – no promises, just challenges and inspiration for me. This was the frontier of the 1960s, one of unlimited and unknown opportunities and perils – a frontier of unfulfilled hopes and threats. Uncharted areas of science and space, unsolved problems of peace and war, unanswered questions of poverty and surplus.

He did not wait for things to happen; he took action to make things happen. He challenged all Americans to choose its future path in 1960, either of the status quo as good as it gets, or to refuse to accept the status quo and achieve the greatness that existed in us and America.

In the world he saw a conflict between freedom and communism and chose to challenge communism. The United States faced a challenge in space that gave an advantage to the Soviet Union for developing nations comparing the relative advantages of capitalism and communism. He stated that there could only be one defense policy for the United States and that was based on the United States as the predominate military and economic power. Not just with military force but with the economic strength of the United States. Economic strength that demonstrated the advantages of freedom over the tyranny of the Soviet Union to the developing nations of the world. He saw economic growth as critical for the future of the United States to lead in space exploration and to eliminate poverty. He proposed and implemented the most significant tax reforms since the new deal – federal policies that encouraged economic growth – including a new tax investment credit. Personal and corporate income taxes were cut to increase incentives and availability of investment capital. He stated that the Federal Government's most useful role is not to rush into a program of excessive increases in public expenditures, but to expand the incentives and opportunities for private expenditures.

In a quote he said, "The cost of freedom is always high, but Americans have always paid it and one path we shall never choose, and that is the path of surrender or submission." He emphasized that in his inaugural address, "Let every nation know, whether it wishes us well or ill, that we shall pay any price, bear any burden support any fried, oppose any foe to assure the survival and success of liberty." He did not shrink from defending freedom but welcomed the responsibility. He saw the need for military might, not to conduct war but to counter any threat that might jeopardize our existence. "It is an unfortunate fact that we can secure peace only by preparing for war."

I remember a leader that searched for solutions – the right thing to do without dwelling on the past but accepting our responsibility for the future. He said that cynics and skeptics were handcuffed in their ability to solve problems because their visions were limited to the obvious realities. Solutions, he said, came from the minds of men that could dream of things that never were. I remember a leader that acted both through the legislature and on his own to improve the lives of Americans, to insure equal rights for all Americans. He challenged Americans to try, even if they failed because those who dare to fail miserably can achieve greatness. He also said that efforts and courage are not enough to achieve results without purpose and direction.
He saw the effects of tyranny and saw how a reluctance to confront tyranny in its early stages created far worse problems in the future.

He also looked to the future when we would match its military strength with our moral restraint, our wealth with our wisdom, our power with our purpose. He saw a world where unconditional war could no longer lead to unconditional victory. It could no longer serve to settle disputes, that we must never negotiate out of fear, but never fear to negotiate.

I saw in John Kennedy the future of America and I had pride in my country and my president. I looked forward to the future envisioned by John Kennedy – not a future that would be handed to us on a silver platter but a future that challenged us to move forward with purpose and direction, to dream, to try even if we failed and try again until we achieved success. I did not just accept his challenge – ask what you can do for your country, I lived it for thirty years.

Chapter 9 – Post JFK

In retrospect, many people speculate what a President Kennedy would have done in the remainder of his presidency had he lived, and I am guilty of that as well. This is essentially an interesting and futile academic exercise with virtually every prognosticator in reality expressing their own opinion of what they would have done. My sole prediction is that he would have acted far more decisively than President Johnson in Vietnam, either in getting involved militarily or withdrawing from Vietnam.

Some questions must be considered. What would have happened if Lee Harvey Oswald had been granted a visa to go back to Cuba? What would have happened to the civil rights legislation proposed by President Kennedy? Would a Vice-President Lyndon Johnson had been as effective a salesman, getting in someone's face and looking up their nose, as a President Johnson?

60 years ago John Fitzgerald Kennedy appeared on the presidential scene and for his most ardent fans, especially me, he has never left that scene. He still lives in my memory and my political being and dreams of what could have been, and he is the standard by which I judge all other presidents – both Democrat and Republican. A quote from President Kennedy was "A man may die, nations may rise and fall, but an idea lives on." For me, the man is John Fitzgerald Kennedy. His life ended but the inspiration of his ideas survives in me, the real man with all of his qualities, good, bad and indifferent, not the myth of Camelot.

Publishing by: Maple Leaf Publishing Inc.
3rd Floor 4915 54 Street
Red Deer, Alberta T4N 2G7, Canada

https://mapleleafpublishinginc.com

To order additional copies of this book, contact:
1-(403)-356-0255

N° ISBN : 978-1-77419-009-8

Rev. date : 06/09/2019

Cover creation : Frédéric Bar

Layout : Frédéric Bar

www.ingramcontent.com/pod-product-compliance
Lightning Source LLC
Chambersburg PA
CBHW061103050726
47592CB00004B/1811